G. William Jones

LANDING RIGHTSIDE UP IN TV & FILM

An Unusual Experience in Screen Media Readiness for Teachers, Churchmen, and Youth-serving Agencies

ILLUSTRATED BY CHARLES COX

ABINGDON PRESS   Nashville and New York

LANDING RIGHTSIDE UP IN TV AND FILM

Copyright © 1973 by Abingdon Press

Library of Congress Cataloging in Publication Data

JONES, GEORGE WILLIAM, 1931-. Landing rightside
up in TV and film. Bibliography: p.   1. Social
work with youth. 2. Church group work with young
adults. 3. Television and youth. 4. Moving-pictures
and youth. I. Title.
HV1421.J64   362.7   72-8270

ISBN 0-687-21047-X

MANUFACTURED BY THE PARTHENON PRESS AT
NASHVILLE, TENNESSEE, UNITED STATES OF AMERICA

To
*All the preachers who know that the Word
is not just words;
all the teachers who try to be midwives
instead of founts of knowledge;
all the youth workers who become co-explorers
rather than fence-keepers.*

I had one great problem in preparing this book: I wanted to write to three distinct groups of people: teachers, churchmen, and leaders in youth-serving agencies, about motion pictures and television as vital adjuncts to their work, but I didn't think that writing three different books was necessary. While there is much common to the three different groups that needs to be understood and experienced, there are, however, three ways of getting into the subject, one of which tends to be rather idiosyncratic with each group. Not wanting to make the churchman plow through the teacher's material, or the youth leader wade through the churchman's concerns, I have used the "branching" technique, which enables each reader to use only those pages that pertain to his particular concern.

A second problem was that I wanted this book to be more like my usual classroom/conference experience than like the monological reading of a book. Therefore, this book is designed so that, in a way, it talks to you and you talk to it—a little two-way communication, hopefully. If the idea of using screen media in your work is something you haven't thought about before, this book may take you an hour or two to read. If you're already "into" the screen media, you'll probably zip through in fifteen minutes. I hope you have a good time with it.

G. W. J.

IF you are primarily concerned about the role of **education** in an age when students spend more time watching films and TV than they spend in the classroom—

turn to page 9.

IF you are primarily concerned about the role of **religion** in an age which is remarkably close, in many ways, to the pre-Gutenbergian days of two or three thousand years ago—

turn to page 11.

IF you are primarily concerned about the role of **youth-serving agencies** in an age when the generation gap gapes wider and wider—

turn to page 13.

IF you are concerned about two or all of these roles— stick around and go through the book several times.

IF you are not concerned about any of these roles— how come you aren't?

It's a warm day. Flies are buzzing against window-panes. Students are sleepy, bored, yearning for the bell to ring. But you want desperately for them to learn something new—to ask a new question, to become terribly excited about a new realization, to click into that wonderful groove of self-motivated inquiry.

Let's say you've been lecturing to them for twenty minutes now, stopping occasionally to see if there are any questions. But there aren't any—so what do you do now?

A. Go ahead, doggedly and bravely, with your lecture, secure in the knowledge that the "truth" is there, if they'll just listen and dig it out? *If you think this is the answer, turn to page 15.*

B. Give up, and ask them about something they *do* seem concerned about, like last weekend's ball game, or the TV show last night? *If you think this is the answer, turn to page 17.*

C. Call a moratorium and hold a little caucus to find out what—in the general area of the subject at hand—they *are* vitally interested in? *If you think this is the answer, turn to page 19.*

Let's say you're a preacher, and you're delivering a sermon you've worked on for at least twenty hours this past week—cutting out all irrelevancies, making sure of a logical progression from point to point, making sure of the facts you marshal to drive these points home—but the whole thing seems dead to you now. They're not really interested out there, they're just being politely quiet until you quit.

Or say you're a Sunday school teacher, and what you thought was going to be a great lesson is not turning out to be that at all—your words feel like ashes in your mouth. You wish your class would respond, perk up, do something!

What do you do now (or at least by next Sunday)?

A. Stick it out, make it to the end, and you've done your duty so that you can all go home and relax? *See page 21, if you think this.*

B. Tell a joke—the first one you can think of (a clean one, of course)—to break the monotony and restore a little life? *See page 23, if you think this.*

C. Resolve next time to tell a story. Wrap up what you want to say in a narrative of everyday life and everyday people? *If you think this, see page 25.*

You want to talk to your group about something very important. You need to talk to them, and you think they need to hear what you have to say. But they don't seem to think so. Everything seems OK as long as your conversation with them is "Hi! How was school today?" or "Hey! That's a sharp outfit you've got on there. Going somewhere special?" But when you really want to discuss something serious with them, they get this distant, uneasy, vaguely irritated look, and your words don't seem to carry your meanings and feelings over to them very well.

What do you do now?

A. Raise your voice a little to indicate how important this is, how much you feel it, and to be sure you hold their attention? *See page 27.*

B. Let it go for now. Approach them about it later, when they seem more open, more receptive? *See page 29.*

C. Admit that you're a little uncertain and uneasy yourself, and try to indicate that it's a problem you all have, and you need to find a way *together* to look at it? *See page 31.*

Well, as long as you're in the middle of this situation, you may *have* to tough it out until the end of the hour. But your attitude seems to smack of an "it isn't education unless it's painful" theory, whereas most educational researchers and theorists today tell us that learning is in the hands of the learner, and that he only chooses to learn that which seems relevant to his existence as it is right now. Next time, try a different approach. Right now, *go back to page 9 and try a different answer.*

That kind of a gambit may work nicely once or twice a semester, but if you fall into it regularly, (1) people will think you're one of the ones who completely misunderstood the "progressive education" movement (old hat now, anyway) and (2) your students will soon know that they can get "old So-and-so" off the track into an irrelevant bull session any time they please. There is one good possibility here, however—that is, if the TV show last night had something relevant to what you've been lecturing about. TV is a hot line into the attention of your students. But perhaps you'd better *go back to page 9 and pick another, better alternative.*

Bravo! You're doing something that avoids the suicidal stubbornness of driving that dead mule of a lecture, and you're also avoiding retreating into the "Marty cop-out" (remember Marty, in the movie— "What do you want to do, Marty?" "I dunno, what do *you* want to do?"), which is a surrender to irrelevance. What you have chosen to do may open some doors, may provide an honestly critical basis upon which to rearrange the curriculum so that it strikes the warm spots of their interest rather than the cold spots of their unconcern. *Go on to page 33.*

Wouldn't it be better just to run screaming from the classroom or pulpit rather than to do this? At least you could admit defeat to your people rather than seem to make a virtue out of boredom. They might take a new view of you if you admitted you were being boring—and something might come out of such openness. But for now, *you'd better turn back to page 11 and pick another alternative.*

Ho-ho-ho! That was a neat little trick you played there. Got the cat off your back for a few minutes, didn't it? Or did it? They may be quite distracted now in trying to figure out what on earth that joke had to do with the subject, or else in being disgusted with you for such an obvious side step—particularly if you now go back to the same old, monotonous lecture. Speaking of going back, *you'd better go back to page 11 and pick another alternative.*

Congratulations! You seem to be one of those who has been interested not only in *what* Jesus and the prophets had to say, but also in *how* he and some of the prophets said it. "Without a parable spoke he not unto them." And what is a parable but a little story of everyday life which illustrates a point, rather than trying to make it propositionally? And boringly? A proposition is boring because it forces you as the listener into a passive learning stance—you can only accept or reject a proposition. But a parable, that's different. You wrestle with it until it yields up its meaning to you. Now *that's* kind of exciting, providing each hearer gets to do it for himself. *Turn to page 35. You're doing fine.*

What happens when your voice volume goes up? Your listeners' hearing goes down, and maybe their respect with it. You've "blown your cool"—a terrible thing to do in the eyes of contemporary youth. (Incidentally, audiovisual researchers have discovered that attention *decreases* with a rise in volume, and vice versa.) *Better go back to page 13 and pick another answer.*

What makes you think there'll ever be a better time, or that they'll ever be in a more receptive mood than now? Dreamer! Don't put off talking with them just because they're not hanging on your every word, licking your face, etc. They know you have something important to say (that's why they're getting uneasy)—but their idea of you isn't going to get any better if you always chicken out and put it off. *Go back to page 13 and pick a better answer.*

You've done this before, haven't you? Or else you have the imagination to put yourself in their shoes. If there's anything that turns them off, it's being faced with an "I know all about it, but you know nothing at all" attitude. They appreciate, however, being accepted as fellow human beings. Besides, they already know that *you* have problems, too. So you're certainly off on the right foot when you take a "self-revealing" stance with them rather than an "advice-giving," or "issue-evading" stance. *Go on to page 37.*

Let's say that you do have a no-holds-barred, brain-storming session in which your students are able to bring up all aspects of your current area of study that they are vitally interested in. Perhaps a list on the blackboard (or an overhead transparency, if you've already phased out those old-fashioned blackboards) has grown to eight or ten items. What do you do now with these valuable clues to the vital interests of your students?

A. Plan a new series of lectures on the basis of these clues, lectures which will really hit the spot now? *Go to page 39.*

B. Drag out all your film catalogues and guides to upcoming TV programs and see what you can find that is related to these interests? *Go to page 41.*

C. Start a series of discussions on these topics, with yourself as a storehouse of knowledge, ready to impart needed facts or to make corrections when the discussion goes wrong? *See page 43.*

Having made a decision to try out the parable (or parabolic) approach to communicating with your congregation or class, you may find it rather difficult to make up parables that fulfill the qualifications of brevity, conciseness, and elicitiveness of response. You may start looking around for some sources of modern parables which are close at hand, not easily used up, and (preferably) in a medium that is already a favorite with your people. Where do you look?

A. To newspaper and magazine articles of actual events which can be used as parables? *See page 45.*

B. To the latest movies that most everyone has seen, to the favorite TV shows, or to short films that can be used in the sanctuary or classroom—sort of "visual parables"? *See page 47.*

C. To the many books of sermon illustrations which have been available for years, and which contain many little stories, anecdotes, and quotations that will serve as parables? *See page 49.*

OK, so you're going to try to put yourself on an even level with your bunch; or, rather you're going to admit that you're in the same boat with them, in that *you* have problems, too—perhaps very like the ones they have. How do you find some sort of common ground with them, a place to stand that is equally interesting and relevant to all of you? Something all of you have a willingness, and even eagerness, to talk about?

A. Hearken back to the time when you were their age. Perhaps you had something of the same problem they're having now. Tell them how you worked it out back then. *See page 51.*

B. Think about the movies or television programs you've seen that they are likely to have seen, too. Perhaps there are some dramatic depictions of similar problems in them you can use in talking about the problem. *See page 53.*

C. Try to recall some news item of a recent event which might illustrate the problem or give a possible answer to it. Perhaps they will have read this, too, and it can become a conversational platform for all of you. *Go to page 55.*

Whoa! You're getting back into the same old bag! A lecture on a topic which is admittedly interesting to your pupils is a lot better than a lecture on something they consider irrelevant, but it's still a lecture; and you're still forcing them to sit back and let *you* do all the thinking, creating, deciding—and talking. *Go back to page 33 and pick a better answer.*

I admire your perspicacity! Obviously you know that this new generation is a visually oriented generation, and that films and television constitute a "hot line" into their attention (and, if into their attention, then almost automatically into their concern). If you can possibly couch your educational goals within relevant films they have seen in the theatre, shorter films you can bring into the classroom, or television programs they can watch at home (or if the time is right, even in class), you're already burrowing inexorably into their centers of concern and relevance.

Go on to page 57.

Discussions are great learning experiences—*providing* they are well led and do not become a mere "pooling of ignorance." A great part of their being well led is making sure that *everyone*, and not just the leader, is a potential source of knowledge on the subject at hand. Leaping unprepared into a discussion—even on a very interesting topic—invites the blahs of shallow thinking and conclusion-leaping. *Better go back to page 33 for another choice.*

Better go back to page 33 for another choice.

Actual events may make some of the strongest and most compelling parables. However, newspaper and magazine articles about news events strive for a very objective and impersonal style of reporting, whereas the power of parables, to a great extent, lies in their subjective and revealingly personal ways of interpreting events. News reports give largely external and large-scale views of life and the world, while parables usually give inside and small-scale views of life and the world. *Go back to page 35 and pick another possibility.*

What on earth made you think of movies or television—right here in the *church* of all places? Tsk, tsk. Seriously, though, you're really on target. The screen arts of motion pictures and television are probably the best sources of parables in our contemporary situation. In the best productions offered to us on the large and small screens we have little stories of lifelike people in lifelike situations. The meanings of these stories are left implicit and concrete, so that we viewers may make these meanings explicit, and draw abstract understandings from them—which is what parables are made for. Not only that, but the screen arts of our visual age are close at hand, not easily used up, and in two media that are already favorite forms of communication for most of your people. *Go on to page 59.*

Ho-hum! Although sermon illustrations have become very popular over the last fifty years of preaching, they most often bear little relationship to parables. A sermon illustration is a mocked-up story or quip, with only one possible interpretation, designed to hammer home the preacher's point; whereas a parable is an open-ended story, which—in its "gracious ambiguity"—has many possible interpretations, any number of which may be "correct" for the individual hearer. *Go back to page 35 and choose again, please.*

Oh my, here comes the old "when I was a boy back in the winter of aught six, I walked five miles to school with bleeding feet" routine. Or so your group will hear it. Frankly, they're not that interested in ancient history, and are likely to feel that conditions have changed so radically since your adolescence that any stories of your own youth are immaterial and totally unrelated to their problems and aspirations. *Better try something else on page 37.*

Now you're really getting with it! Some of the best movies and TV shows of today are doing a great job of dealing with our universal problems and confusions in a revealing and depth-probing manner. If you and your group can't talk of your personal hang-ups in a direct way, you can certainly try using similar situations in something you've both seen recently on a screen (large or small) as sort of indirect "mirror images" of your experiences. *Go on to page 61.*

I'm sorry, just as you are, I guess, that youth don't read the newspapers as much as we adults do. Oh, they know what's happening on the campuses and streets very well, and a few of them are "news-hogs"; but with the greater number of youth, you won't find much common ground in trying to discuss the latest national and international news events. This is not to say that they are dull or unconcerned—far from it! It's just that the main occupational task of an adolescent is the search for identity in the small world of direct relationships. The task of relating to the big world of national and international events comes a little later.

Caveat: A lot of adolescents are getting into the bag of protest today; but for the youngest majority of them, even this is more a matter of the search for personal identity, over against handed-down values and the power system, rather than an altruistic attempt to change society.

So how about going back to page 37 to pick an alternative?

Now that you've decided that the "eyes" have it for young students of today, and you're going to try to utilize motion pictures and television as a means of helping ideas and concerns to sprout and blossom, your task has not ended, it has just taken a new direction. Many screen presentations can be just as boring to a group of students as a lecture. (There's not much magic in the medium *per se* for these kids who have had unlimited and immediate access to television since before they can remember.) The crucial point lies in your *selection* of a TV program, film clip, or short film which is relevant to your educational topic or concern, creative in itself, and productive of emotional and intellectual struggle within each pupil. How do you begin to find this kind of material?

A. Check with your local public library or nearest university to see if they have a catalogue of "experimental" films (sometimes called art films), then find some way to view as many of them as you can. Also, get your local network TV stations to put you on their mailing lists for advance program information. *Go to page 63.*

B. Find out all the local resources for educational films, and run through the appropriate categories in their subject catalogues; then try to get on the advance program information mailing list of your local educational TV channel. *Go to page 65.*

C. Call upon someone who knows more about TV and film than you do to find and select things for you. *Go to page 67.*

Once having decided that the screen arts, as represented by today's motion pictures and television, can be an ally to you rather than just a traditional enemy, you face a new problem. Which films and television programs will help your group to come to the most realistic, creative, and discerning understandings of the challenge of today's world to our religious ministries? How do you begin to uncover these resources?

A. Get catalogues from all the distributors of religious films in your area, then write to the director of religious programming of the networks to ask for advance information on upcoming religious TV programs? *Go to page 69.*

B. Contact your local public library or nearest university for catalogues of their experimental films (sometimes referred to as "art" films); secure catalogues as well from your nearest distributors of entertainment films. Then ask your local network stations to put you on their advance program information mailing lists. *Turn to page 71.*

C. Get a person (perhaps in your own congregation) who works in television or films, or who studied them in college, or who makes films as a hobby, to be your advisor for the selection of appropriate films and TV programs. *Go to page 73.*

Now *which* motion pictures and TV programs are most likely to provide a good basis for discussing some of your mutual concerns? It's not the visual media *per se* that are interesting and exciting for youth, but only the productions of the visual media they consider to be the most relevant and meaningful. Which of the following kinds of screen productions do you think would make the best discussion-starters for you and your group?

A. The very few family films of today, which no one would have any qualms about taking even their youngest children to see? *See page 75.*

B. The rather disturbing—and often erotic or critical of the status quo—films which teenagers seem for varying reasons to be flocking to see? *Go to page 77.*

C. The fine "message" pictures which present a clear and forthright statement of some moral, religious, or patriotic precepts? *See page 79.*

It is very interesting that you should have chosen the experimental, or art, films and network television —and very correct, from my point of view. The beauty of the best of the experimental films (such as *Adventures of ** or *A Time out of War*) is that they are highly creative both in form and in content, and are viewer-involving by virtue of their *openness*. They tend to raise questions rather than give pat answers, and to elicit attitudes of awe and wonder rather than those of mere acceptance and finality. If you are concerned with the arts and humanities, these are the best films for your purposes, so *go on to page 81;* but if you teach science, perhaps you'd best *go back to page 57 and choose* B.

If you are primarily concerned with teaching subjects like math or chemistry—the sciences—then this probably is a good choice, because the teaching of these subjects, at least, at the present time, tends to require direct and concise materials (such as films like *Hyper-Butyl-Oxy Reactions at 107° Fahrenheit*) found mostly in educational film catalogues and on Educational Television. But don't overlook the possibility of using experimental films, or even entertainment TV programs, which may have an indirect application to your subject. *Go on to page 81.*

However, if you are concerned about teaching the humanities or arts, you may find that most of the educational films and ETV programs are far too uncreative, presenting facts as far too unequivocal and "set" to provoke any spark of creativity or excitement in your students. *Go back to page 57.*

The temptation is strong, when you are faced by a new teaching medium, to throw up your hands and turn it all over to the "experts." The trouble with this attitude, however, is that (1) no outsider can ever know as well as you what your class needs at this moment; and (2) you need to become the expert yourself in choosing and using visual media for your classes. Better get started *now* through the hard—but enjoyable and exciting—process of new learning and trial and error. *So go back to page 57 and pick again.*

If you want to get into meaningful dialogue with some reasonably everyday types of persons, then this is probably the worst choice you could have made. Religious films and TV programs (with a few notable exceptions, such as *Parable, A Time for Burning, These Four Cozy Walls,* etc., on a list that grows slowly), are the most uncreative, unimaginative, uninvolving, and unrealistic productions ever made. By presenting the truth of life in such sentimentalized and simplistic terms as most of them do, you can only convince the moderate realist that religion has very little to do with his everyday life. *Go back to page 59, please.*

It may be that you began utilizing the screen arts in religious programs by using so-called religious films and television and then gave up on them as being totally inadequate and misleading. If so, you may have been amazed at how comparatively relevant, creative, elicitive, and depth-serious some of our so-called secular, or even entertainment, movies and video shows can be when brought into the life of a religious group trying to grapple seriously with life issues. Congratulations, you've made a good choice. *Go on to page 81.*

Just one of the problems we have traditionally faced when religion has attempted to utilize the screen arts is who should design and execute church-produced films. Should we trust the theologian who is an amateur film buff or use the professional screen artist who is an amateur theologian? What we need, of course, is an interdisciplinarian expert who is equally well versed in both theology and the screen arts. And you are one of the likely candidates for this "new breed," even if you only serve to help interpret the best screen arts and get them their deserved attention in the church. So you may learn a lot about film and television from that local screen expert of yours, but don't turn over your responsibilities for wise selection and utilization to him. Start now to become a screen theologian yourself. *Go back to page 59.*

You may get a big honk out of the latest and best G-rated film or seven-o'clock show on the tube—and it may be excellent entertainment—but don't plan on getting many young people excitedly talking about it, at least not on any depth level in regard to serious life concerns. You may occasionally find such a film that doesn't gloss over and sentimentalize real issues, if it deals with them at all; but most are very superficial and designed to entertain and not to confront. Sorry, *go back to page 61.*

Of course! You want to talk with them on the basis of some mutual and recent experiences of screen-viewing, so you will have to be more alert to what today's teen-agers are choosing to watch on the tube and to see in the theatre, not just once, but twice or thrice (what they call "their" films). These are what you're going to have to go see. Some adults may find this fact a bitter pill, and some may be a bit shocked, but these are the screen productions the youth want to talk about; and you won't be able to make much sense trying to talk about them if you haven't seen them.

Let's broaden the picture at this point. We'll say that you need no longer rely only upon what happens to be playing at the local theatre or on TV as grist for your dialogue, but you can also be thinking now of *prearranging* a viewing-dialogue session by finding a good film, getting a projector, and showing the film to your group. *Go on to page 81.*

If your young people are like most of their counter-
parts, you have a problem here. They dislike being
preached at or conned, and the more obvious the
moral or message of the picture (unless it's one *they*
want *you* to get), the less likely they are to respect
the picture or those who liked it.

Better go back to page 61 and choose again.

Once you find a few likely looking productions in film catalogues or advance TV guides, you should try to avoid buying a "pig in a poke" by *previewing* before you order them or advise your group to watch them. Of course, with TV this is well-nigh impossible, with two exceptions: (1) you can keep mental or written notes on the best TV programs you see—what network ran them, what department or company produced them, who directed them, etc. Often advance publicity will cite this information on future programs, and you'll be better able to recommend a program if these same names reappear; and (2) it is possible, but rather unlikely that you can get in on an advance closed-circuit preview of up-coming programs at local TV stations. They usually do this only with "specials," the ones most likely to be controversial, and then only for their own staff and a few news media people. Otherwise, you just have to rely on the sketchy descriptions of content in your advance program notes.

With films it's a different matter. Many public film libraries will send out a film for previewing, or let you come to their offices to preview. If they're reluctant to do this, get several leaders together who are likely to want to use the film for their groups, then make a joint request. A group preview will be worth the library's while and the wear and tear on their preview print. With commercial film libraries you cannot usually preview, but some of them (Films, Inc., for instance) have rather comprehensive discussion guides which will give you a good idea of a film's content and relevance.

What are the elements of paramount importance for which you look when previewing a film for group use?

A. Is it more important that a film be right on the subject, or well-photographed, creative in form and content, and with a crisp and clear sound track? *If you think the first is most important, go to page 85.*
B. Or, is it more important that a film be creative both in its photography and approach to the content, and have a good sound track, just so long as its subject is somewhere within the area of your concern? *If you think this, go to page 87.*
C. Or perhaps the most important thing about a film is its "source credibility," according to the long-term establishment of the film company that produced it, the qualifications of its narrator or consultant, etc. *If this seems most important, go to page 89*

Fifteen or twenty years ago I might have agreed with you. But today "the medium is the message" is not only a catchy motto, but also the truth—especially if you happen to be working with young persons. A film may deal exactly with the subject you feel your group needs right now and still be a poor choice. If a film is poorly photographed, put together with the 1930's style of editing, with no fast cuts, a logical 1-2-3 time sequence, no unannounced switching from reality to what-ifness, etc., and has a badly recorded sound track featuring music that's too heavy and a narrator who's too dramatic, it can turn off your group. Such a film is saying, through these elements, something like "this is an out-of-date attitude toward a topic about which we feel sentimental but not very serious. This is old-hat, and it has very little to do with now-reality. Ho-hum."

Go back to page 83.

An excellent choice, showing valuable insight into just what's happening! An uncreative, old-style film about an important topic has a way of making an audience feel, unconsciously, that the topic itself is outmoded, unworthy of serious consideration, boring, etc. If the subject matter is really important for here and now, the very *form* of the film should say this, too, with the newest and most effective (not just faddish or gimmicky) forms of cinematic expression. These may include fast cuts (only a few frames or a glimpse); jarring switches from present to future to past to future-possible; unannounced switches from reality to fantasy, from external images to internal images; use of color or sound to add a new dimension to the picture, etc. Yes! *Go on to page 91.*

Granted, source credibility is an important factor in some kinds of endeavors, particularly if you're teaching science or trying to help people analyze the contemporary world situation, etc. But what we are mainly concerned with here is "turning on" persons with TV or film so they'll become excited enough and interested enough to begin doing their own thinking and expressing about a concern. Creditable sources can always be added at the right moments on a mimeographed sheet; but for this *elicitative* stage of the game, the "authoritative answer" might tend to turn more persons *off* than *on*. *How about returning to page 83 for another choice?*

Now that you've selected a film or chosen a relevant and creative TV program to alert a group to (or, if the time is right, to view together), you're going to say something about it before they see it. Right? The important—*crucially* important—next question is what kinds of things are most helpful and appropriate as introduction to a viewing experience?

A. A short and simple statement about why you (or your consultants in the group) have chosen to present *this* film at *this* time; i.e., a "bridging" statement between what has been going on in your group and the way this film or TV program is expected to work into the process. But you avoid making any but the most general statements regarding the content. *If this seems right, go to page 93.*

B. A short list of things to look for or things to notice in the film or program, warning the group that these will be the things you'll expect to discuss afterwards. *If this seems right, go to page 95.*

C. A statement about the film's relevance, creativity, and other positive qualities, which you have determined from previewing it and reading catalogue copy and advance notes; mention of the awards it has won and what critics have said, etc. *If this seems a good thing to do, go to page 97.*

Correct! You obviously want to avoid saying anything which will preclude each individual's own judgment of the film or program or make him feel that you're putting him on the spot, so that he'll be nervously searching for the things you've mentioned beforehand. You want him to get as involved in the film as possible while it is running, and then to be as free as possible to draw his own conclusions about its relevance and quality, what it makes him think about, which were the most important and best-done portions, etc. Great! You've helped him to put the film into the perspective of the group's ongoing concerns *without* standing between him and the experience. *Go on to page 99.*

Unless you're working with kids under eleven or twelve years of age, you're doing more harm than good to the group process by doing this. We have experimental evidence that children under eleven or twelve have an extremely difficult time following a film story or line of reasoning, and specific *what-to-look-fors* might help such children in their viewing experience. However, with older children (and even with under-twelves, if the film is a freewheeling, nonlinear "experience" rather than a story or propositional development) you will be superimposing your own interpretation of the film's relevance or meaning if you do this, and probably squelching, to some degree, each person's private response to the film. *Go back to page 91 for another choice.*

What you seem to be trying to do is to bolster the group's opinion of the film (and of you as a film selector) before they see it. This can be a noble effort if, by doing it, you are seeking to help them take the film more seriously and thus derive more benefit from the viewing. But the proof of the screen arts lies in the seeing, and the ideal plan would seem to be to let each person come to his *own* judgment of the production's relevance and quality. After all, if you and the professional critics say how great the thing is and he doesn't agree, he'll probably lapse into a frustrated silence, rather than feeling free and open about his responses. You don't want that, do you? *If not, go back to page 91.*

You're ready to view! Of course, some hours ago, you made sure that the TV set or film projector was in fine working order (and that extra projection and exciter bulbs were on hand for the projector, plus a spare drive-spring in case one breaks during the screening), and you've arranged the screen and chairs so that everyone has an unimpeded view. You've tested the sound for the room—remembering that bodies absorb sound, and so a room when full of people requires a higher volume and has less reverberation than when empty. The film is properly threaded into the projector, and any extra reels are kept close at hand, etc. Between now and the end of the program or film, is there anything else you can do that will make the experience more creative, elicitive, and stimulating?

A. No, just make sure that sight and sound are kept at optimum levels until the program or film is over. *See page 101.*

B. Yes, you can turn down the volume at times to make some elucidative comments of your own. *See page 103.*

C. Yes, you can stop the film at appropriate places (or take advantage of commercial breaks) to ask for some up-to-now comments or questions from the group. *See page 105.*

A. If it's a tightly knit dramatic film you're viewing, with no real stopping places that wouldn't mar the unity of the experience, you're right. But for TV programs and other kinds of films, you really ought to *go back to page 99 for another choice.*

B. They're going to hate you if you do this! In the first place, they will be frustrated at missing what's being shown and said while you're talking; and in the second place, they may find you a bit pompous to be "explaining" the production to them—or even appearing to do so. Don't try this except with a silent film—and then only gingerly and very humbly. *Go back to page 99.*

C. Very creative of you! Unless you want the commercials themselves to be an object of discussion later, this is an excellent way to make the most of the one- to three-minute breaks in the program's continuity. And if it's a film, who says you have to show it all at once, just because it's all in one string? Be free! Experiment! Remember Kino-Automat at Expo, and try a "what would *you* do now?" approach, or try showing just the most relevant sections, or try stopping for questions and comments at places you've preselected and which don't damage the flow of the film. *Go on to page 107.*

"The End" flashes on the screen, and you turn off the set or the projector. Now what? We've begun this entire enterprise because you wanted a more effective means of communicating with your group, a more relevant means, which would be more likely to draw out each person's own thoughts, ideas, and feelings and get him dramatically involved in a free and open discussion. Well, now's the time! This is what it has all been for.

Relatively few films or TV programs need no follow-up discussion and are sufficient in themselves as creativity "inputs" (like Norman McLaren's abstract animations) or are so deeply moving or soul-cracking that discussion invariably seems to be a sacrilege (like Alain Resnais' *Night and Fog*). With these you have to wait until later—sometimes *much* later—to discuss them. Except in these few cases, the discussion of a film or TV program is the intellectual and emotional digestion of it. Without discussion afterwards, the vicarious experience of a screen production tends to evaporate very quickly, like a dream when you're awakened. So how do you capture the greatest benefit of a film or program in follow-up discussion?

A. Give your own summary and interpretation of what has been screened; then ask the others for any additional or differing points? *If you think so, see page 111.*

B. Pick out specific events or symbols in the film and ask the group members to give their interpretations of them, along the lines of your group's main concerns? *If this seems right, see page 113.*

C. Just let the people bring up whatever they want to about the film or program, and don't attempt to guide the discussion at all? *If this, see page 115.*

D. Have on hand some questions that you prepared after previewing the film, or a discussion guide that has some suggestions for discussion which are genuine questions (and not thinly veiled statements with question marks at the ends). Use the questions that seem most stimulating to the group as discussion-starters, letting questions from the group itself always have preference? *If you would do this, see page 117.*

There you go, smothering the other persons' own, individual responses! If you're the leader of the group, or the senior member, in age, etc., the others are just likely to let it go at that and not offer any of their own interpretations or feelings about the screen presentation. They'll be too polite, threatened, or bored to go up against your interpretation. Silence will reign. The same thing will happen if you ask "leading" questions, or succumb too often to the delicious temptation to answer your own questions. *Go back to page 109.*

This is a good way to squeeze the life out of a film—or a group. When a film has been creative, open-ended, perhaps very artistically and evocatively ambiguous (like life), it is very heavy-handed, and perhaps even irreverent, to "symbol-monger" or intellectualize it until it has all been dissected and defused. This can be a way of hiding from the real import and impact which the film can have; a way of "pulling its teeth," by putting it all in safe and comfortable pigeonholes. Don't do it. *For a better way, go back to page 109 and choose again.*

If you have a group which is already very sophisticated about viewing and discussing screen experiences, you may not be taking too great a risk. But otherwise, you risk having a muddy pooling of irrelevancies, heavy-handed interpretations and summaries, arguments over fine points of little concern to the total group—and embarrassing silences. This can be a good gambit after the discussion has gotten well started into profitable and revealing pathways, but not to begin with. *Go back to page 109.*

You have the right idea for the large majority of these occasions. You only have to be continually careful to (1) use questions which are *really* questions and not discussion squelching statements like "don't you think that so-and-so should have done such-and-such?"; (2) be sensitive to good questions which emerge from group members themselves, for they are often more profitable than the "canned" questions from discussion guides; (3) be cool, after you pose a question, and give them time to think and react; don't get nervous and leap in to answer the question yourself or scurry to the next question; and (4) be sure to discuss both content and form—not only *what* the screen production had to express, but *how* it expressed it to you. *Go on to page 119.*

It has been great threading through this maze of choices and decisions with you. I hope it has helped you to think of some new things you can do that will be of genuine aid to you and your group as you try to "land rightside up in TV and film." If it has all been old stuff to you, then I (a) apologize for having aimed too low in trying to design a reading experience for a "general" audience (whatever that is); (b) rejoice to find another practicing screen-education enthusiast; and (c) promise to do better in the future.

As a last act, perhaps you'll do a little evaluation of how well I've communicated with you in these pages. If you had to put into just a sentence or two what you've understood this booklet to be driving at, it would be something like:

A. The screen media of TV and the movies are so intrinsically stimulating and communicative that almost any film is bound to be more effective—especially with the young—than any lecture type presentation. *If this is what you've "heard," go to page 121.*

B. Any facet of any subject can be communicated best by a wise use of TV-film. *If this sounds like it, go to page 123.*

C. "The film's the thing"—a student by himself with the right film is better off than a student in a classroom with only a teacher, classmates, and his books. *If this is it, go to page 125.*

D. Film and television, when they are creative and open-ended, and followed by stimulating discussion, can be one of the most exciting and effective means of discovery and communication available to us today. *If this seems to be it, turn to page 127.*

A. I'm sorry. I didn't mean to give you any grounds for interpreting what I had to say in that way. We can never afford to forget—even with all the emerging forms of communication—that there are great lectures and there are poor screen presentations, and the former is always better than the latter. (But this doesn't let great lecturers off the hook, for they'll do even better in cahoots with great works of screen art!) For what I *did* mean to express, *go back to page 119 and read* D.

B. Either I miswrote or you misread, or we each did a
a little of both. A"wise use of TV-film" requires
restraint and an eagle eye for those goals best accomplished by the use of the screen, and those
best accomplished by discussion, lecture, role playing, field trips, research, etc. Whenever a new
means of communication has emerged, people
have always been afraid it would supplant preexist-
ing media. But we still talk, read, listen to the radio,
etc. *For what I did mean, go back to page 119 and
read D.*

C. Although it sounds like something a present-day Martin Luther might have said, I consider it dead wrong. As I wrote on page 107, the digestive discussion following a screen presentation is a vital part of the screen experience, without which the experience tends to evaporate. And such discussion requires a group and a sensitive and well-prepared leader. *What I did mean to say is on page 119,* D.

D. Right! Welcome to the electro-visual age!

For Further Exploration

Boutwell, William D. *Using Mass Media in the Schools.* New York: Appleton-Century-Crofts, 1962.

Hurley, Neil P. *Theology Through Film.* New York: Harper & Row, 1970.

Jones, G. William. *Dialogue with the World.* Chicago: Films, Inc., 1965.

————. *Sunday Night at the Movies.* Richmond: John Knox Press, 1967.

Konzelman, Robert G. *Marquee Ministry.* New York: Harper & Row, 1972.

Kuhns, William, and Stanley, Robert. *Exploring the Film.* With Teaching Program. Dayton: George A. Pflaum, Inc., 1968.

Lindgren, Ernest. *The Art of the Film.* Rev. ed. New York: The Macmillan Company, 1963.

McKeown, Clark, and Sparke, William. *It's Only a Movie.* With Teacher's Manual. Englewood Cliffs, N. J.: Prentice-Hall, 1972.

Mast, Gerald. *A Short History of the Movies.* New York: Pegasus, 1971.

Maynard, Richard A. *The Celluloid Curriculum.* New York: Hayden Press, 1971.

Postman, Neil. *Television and the Teaching of English.* New York: Appleton-Century-Crofts, 1961.

Sheridan, Marion D.; Owen, H. H.; Macrorie, K.; and Marcus, Fred. *The Motion Picture and the Teaching of English.* New York.: Appleton-Century-Crofts, 1962.

Solomon, Stanley. *The Film Idea.* New York: Harcourt Brace Jovanovich, 1972.